A Bat Cannot Bat, a Stair Cannot Stare

More about Homonyms and Homophones

To my parents, Sue (not Sioux) and Mike (not mic).   —B.P.C.

To Patrick Gignac, in all friendship   —M.G.

Homonyms:
two or more words that are pronounced the same and spelled the same but have different meanings

Homophones:
two or more words that are pronounced the same but have different spellings and different meanings

A Bat Cannot Bat, a Stair Cannot Stare

More about Homonyms and Homophones

by Brian P. Cleary

illustrations by Martin Goneau

M MILLBROOK PRESS / MINNEAPOLIS

Homonyms are spelled the same,

and they're alike in sound.

4

Their meanings, though, are different—like

"That sink may sink into the ground."

Or "There's no amount
that a count cannot count."

"I'll tire from
fixing this tire."

"Some down may drift down from a fine feathered gown."

"The steer should steer clear of the fire."

7

A bat cannot bat,
as you need arms for that.

But a batter might
batter some batter.

A mole with a mole could
emerge from his hole

to mop up the splash
and the splatter.

9

And fans could bring fans
to cool off in the stands.

One might watch her
watch for the time.

I may eat a prune,
while I prune, around noon,
two trees that grow
lemons and limes.

Homophones will sound alike:

They're words like blew and blue.

12

Their spellings aren't
the same, you'll see.

Their meanings
differ, too.

A hare can have hair.

And a fare can be fair.

And your feet can accomplish a feat.

A cent can be sent to a gent with the scent of potatoes and onions and meat.

A brake might just break.
It can rattle and shake.

And four can yell "fore!"
for a warning.

If the doctor can **write**
your prescription quite **right**,
he'll heal your **heel** by
morning.

A knight in the night
with the might of a mite
might light up a
castle that's dark.

A sail on sale
could falter and flail.

The doorway can
arc on an ark.

Your hair we can tease
in our T's if we please.
You can sample some
teas or a muffin

Tees & Such

Tease & Toes

or shop at your ease
where they sell balls and tees
and bags to put all your
golf stuff in.

A throne can be thrown (with a grunt and a groan) by mussels with muscles to spare.

WOOO

If the king THREW a SWord,
it Would not be ignored
as it Sailed and Soared
through the air.

But Rome cannot roam,
'cause it has to stay home.

And chili is mostly not chilly.

A base can't play bass.

And with no eyes or face,
a stair cannot stare at
you, silly.

If a seven-toed toad
would be towed down the road
and you rowed a boat
near there to see,

You could peer from the pier at the towed toad seen here in the truck as it rode past the sea.

See how they're funny?
And silly? And punny?
Like, "oh great! Let's
grate some more cheese!"

The fun doesn't lessen as you laugh through each lesson. So why don't you make some of these?

What are homonyms and homophones?

Homonyms

WORD	MEANING 1	MEANING 2
bat	a flying animal	a thick stick or club
down	a covering of soft fluffy feathers	in or going toward a low place
mole	an animal that lives mostly underground	a mark on the skin
prune	a dried plum	to cut off some of the branches of a tree or bush so that it looks better
sink	a wide bowl that has a faucet for water and a drain at the bottom	to go below the surface or to the bottom
steer	a type of ox	to move or guide something in a particular direction or along a path
tire	to lose energy	a rubber cushion that fits around a wheel
watch	to look at	a device that shows what time it is and is worn on the wrist

Do you know?

Homophones

WORD 1	MEANING 1	WORD 2	MEANING 2
arc	a line or shape that is curved like part of a circle	ark	a type of boat
base	the bottom of something, one of the four stations at the corners of a baseball infield	bass	having a low sound, especially for an instrument such as a guitar or drum
brake	something used to slow down or stop movement	break	to stop working correctly
fair	right or honest	fare	money a person pays to travel on a plane, bus, boat, or train, or in a taxi—or the person who pays the money
feat	a big accomplishment	feet	the body parts you stand on
muscle	a body part that helps with movement	mussel	a type of shellfish with a long dark shell
peer	to look at	pier	a structure that goes out from shore into the water
sail	a piece of cloth that catches the wind to move a boat through water	sale	selling something, often at a cheap price

Find activities, games, and more at
www.brianpcleary.com

ABOUT THE AUTHOR AND THE ILLUSTRATOR

Brian P. Cleary is the author of the best-selling Words Are CATegorical©
series, as well as the Math Is CATegorical©, Food Is CATegorical™, Animal Groups
Are CATegorical™, Adventures in Memory™, Poetry Adventures, and Sounds Like
Reading© series. He has also written Do You Know Dewey? Exploring the Dewey
Decimal System, Six Sheep Sip Thick Shakes: And Other Tricky Tongue Twisters,
and several other books. Mr. Cleary lives in Cleveland, Ohio.

MARTIN GONEAU is the illustrator of the Food Is CATegorical™ and Animal
Groups Are CATegorical™ series. He lives in Trois-Rivières, Québec.

Text copyright © 2014 by Brian P. Cleary
Illustrations copyright © 2014 by Lerner Publishing Group, Inc.

Millbrook Press
A division of Lerner Publishing Group, Inc.
241 First Avenue North
Minneapolis, MN 55401 USA

For reading levels and more information, look up this title at www.lernerbooks.com.

Main body text set in RandumTEMP 35/48. Typeface provided by House Industries.

Library of Congress Cataloging-in-Publication Data

Cleary, Brian P., 1959—
    A bat cannot bat, a stair cannot stare : more about homonyms and homophones / by Brian P. Cleary ;
Illustrated by Martin Goneau.
      pages   cm. — (Words Are CATegorical)
    ISBN 978—0—7613—9032—9 (lib. bdg. : alk. paper)
    ISBN 978—1—4677—4768—4 (eBook)
    1. English language—Homonyms—Juvenile literature. I. Goneau, Martin, illustrator. II. Title.
PE1595.C584 2014
    428'.1—dc23   2013030878

Manufactured in the United States of America
1 — DP — 7/15/14